Generis
PUBLISHING

AF722411

FOREIGN INVESTMENT IN THE MINING SECTOR IN AFRICA A FOCUS ON CHINA IN SHURUGWI ZIMBABWE

CHIDO T CHIPFAKACHA

Title: **FOREIGN INVESTMENT IN THE MINING SECTOR IN AFRICA A FOCUS ON CHINA IN SHURUGWI ZIMBABWE**

ISBN: 979-8-89966-465-6

Author: CHIDO T CHIPFAKACHA

Cover image: AI Generated

Publisher: Generis Publishing
Online orders: www.generis-publishing.com
Contact email: info@generis-publishing.com

Foreign Investment in the mining sector in Africa: A Focus on China in Shurugwi Zimbabwe

Chido T Chipfakacha BSc Politics and Public Management

CONTENTS

ABSTRACT

This book is a full blown version of an article which was published by the African Journal of Political Science (AJPS) titled Chinese Funding: A Curse to Africa: A Case of Shurugwi Zimbabwe, the success of the article has inspired the research to be carried on a large scale as will be shown in this book. The relationship of China and many African nations has its roots deeper than the BRICS (Brazil, Russia, India, China and South Africa) bloc and the emergence of the South-South Relations as it is deeply trenched in the role of China in providing ideological and military aid to combat colonization. This book through qualitative and quantitative research outcomes aims to show foreign investment in the mining sector in Africa, with a focus on China in Shurugwi Zimbabwe however it will also aim to show how Chinese investment has dealt a blow to Western monopoly in African economics they by increasing industrial competitiveness that Africans are to take advantage of if they are to develop. The book aim to show the ugly side of Chinese mining in Shurugwi Zimbabwe through a research that has taken four years, the objectives being to protect and create awareness on the dangers of unaccountable government policies. The environment, the society and the economy of Shurugwi and Zimbabwe at large were the main reasons writing for this book as they bleed from Chinese open cast mining.

CHAPTER 1.
INTRODUCTION.
SHURUGWI ZIMBABWE

Shurugwi a victim of mining activities for over a century from the days of the BSAC (British Southern African Company), then the Union Carbide, Anglo American and now the Chinese dominate the town. Shurugwi has a huge historical significance in Zimbabwe as at one time it was home of two nemesis the then Prime Minister of Rhodesia Ian Douglas Smith who resided at Gwenhoro farm in Shurugwi and the man who was among the black Africans that fought to liberate the black majority from the evil minority regime of Ian Smith the distinguished Josiah Magamba Tongogara who was a commander of ZANLA (Zimbabwe African National Liberation Army). Shurugwi is a small town situated 36 km from Gweru which is one of the 5 major cities in Zimbabwe located in the Midlands province at the heart of the mineral rich Great Dyke of Zimbabwe; it is home to many minerals including the one of the largest platinum and chrome deposits in the world. But in recent years they have been a gold rush that has become the source of living for the locals and people from all walks of life in Zimbabwe. The indigenization policy in Zimbabwe driven by the then Mugabe government saw the increase of black ownership of mines in Shurugwi with ZIMASCO which was the biggest holder of mining land in Zimbabwe ceding 50% of 45900 hectares of the land to the government to cater for new investors (Makichi T 2016). In 2007 the acquisition of ZIMASCO by the Chinese mining giant SINO Steel (Bloomberg 2014) brought the Chinese to the forefront of Shurugwi mining. With the coming into power of the government of the 2nd Republic led by President Emmerson Mnangagwa came an influx of Chinese miners with interest in gold mining and as the days went by they began to buy mines from locals with rumors of coercion being used especially using corridors of power.

Below Map of Shurugwi Gold claims before Indigenisation

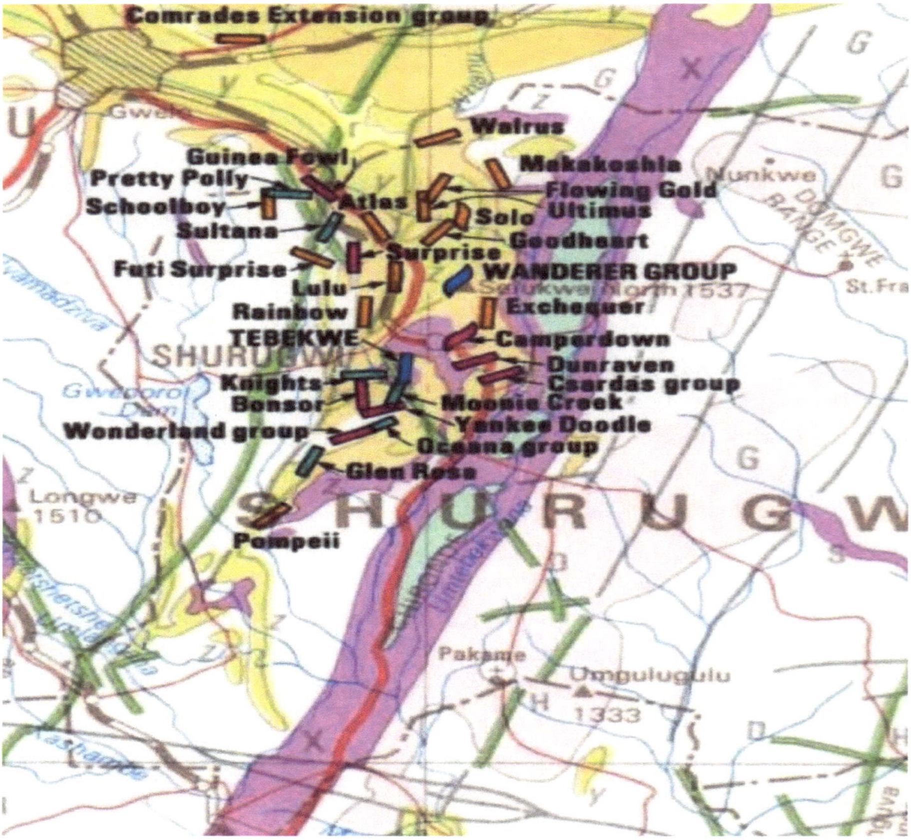

China and Africa Economies Introduction

China`s GDP has experienced one of the miracles of the century from an agricultural economy that superseded the industrial revolution to a world economic superpower whom at one time was rumored to have a surplus of US dollars. The Chinese economy like the economies of most East Asian countries are renowned for growing without Western influence but on their own. China has launched an aggressive economic drive that saw its economy grow by 5% which was the government`s target of 2024 as reported by novanews.pro (2025), this growth pattern has been as a result of a massive investment by the Communist Party in China Inland and in emerging Markets. Africa as a whole has had a few success stories economically with mainly Botswana, South Africa, Rwanda and mostly the Arab North African countries being the most stable countries. West Africa has been the most unstable regions due to military actions like coups and civil wars; this ground has made it a ground for modern plundering by both the East and the West. Burkina Faso, Mali and Niger`s military governments have been praised for breaking the French hold in West Africa, though at what cost? Remain to be answered. The imbalance between trade among the Chinese and its African partners has been a worry on skeptics of these relationships as they see China as taking advantage of the corrupt African states which it mainly trades with. Chinese interests have mainly been in mining and the preferred method being the barbaric open cast mining that is an enemy of the environment. In Zimbabwe the Chinese have been viewed as a threat to policies that had empowered Africans and had answered the grievances of the liberation struggle. The book aims to bring in to light the challenges Africa today faces in the presence of neo-colonialism.

Historical Background of Zimbabwe

Zimbabwe is one of the 16 SADC countries with a rich history spanning centuries from the Great Zimbabwe days to the conquest of the Mutapa State against the Portuguese who failed to colonize them. The country attained its independence from British colonial rule in 1980 after a protracted guerrilla warfare that was ended by the signing of the Lancaster House Agreement but the white colonial government of Ian Douglas Smith and the leaders of the Guerrilla movement mainly ZIPRA (Zimbabwe People`s Revolutionary Army) and ZANLA (Zimbabwe African National Liberation Army). The Chinese were influential in training the liberation movements especially those under the banner of the frontline states and this is a date that Africa thought would one day not be collected. As the African States have tried to move from the grasp of its colonial masters the Chinese and its allies under the guise of South- South relations have begun to fill the void and in some cases to rival the West in areas of economic interest across Africa. The West after the attainment of African States independence have maintained a grip on relations through its Britton wood Institutions of the IMF and World Bank whose policies have proven the truth in Walter Rodney`s book how Europe Underdeveloped Africa. Kwame Nkrumah after the Independence of Ghana wrote that Africa would be recolonized in what is termed neo-colonialism where the colonizers will come as investors though Nkrumah`s theory was mainly concerned with the West it forgot to foresee the Chinese and Eastern bloc that was an all-weather friend for Africa at that time forgetting that they are no permanent friends in the international system but it was a game of interest. Chinese investments in Africa has eclipsed many expectations as they are growing at a rate that has never been experienced in Africa since the scramble of Africa at the

Berlin Conference of 1885 where Africa was divided and shared on a table without it being represented.

The rise in summits between the continent of Africa and individual states has been another disrespect that shows no one takes Africa serious; we have the USA- Africa Summit, Russia-Africa Summit, China-Africa Summit to name a few showing that most countries do not see the capacity of African States as individual states but they prefer putting them under one bracket. It will be unfair analysis to start this work with showing the negative and positive effects of China Africa Relations without pointing out the seed that was planted by the colonial era and in the Zimbabwean case the British and its system which was led in the beginning by one of the most famous plunderers Africa has ever seen Cecil John Rhodes of the BSAC (British Southern African Company). The Chinese-Africa Trade Relations has brought a new dimension and competitiveness in trade in Africa which has been predominantly Western dominated mainly by Transnational Companies this has also brought with it an increase in the allegations of bribery to government officials by the Western and Chinese companies as they wrestle for trade agreements. Glencore International is one Western company that has been found wanting in connection with bribery and Chinese companies have stood up above the rest as will be shown in this book with qualitative references substantiating the evidence.

Brief History on Chinese Loans

Hans Morgenthau (1948) `s theory that states pursue power and interests in an anarchic international system have never been right as the aggressive Chinese foreign policy on trade mainly with 3rd world countries. From having trade relations with people whom the West on moral grounds would not trade with like the Taliban and North Korea known for their track records on Human Rights. The Chinese have become a major rival of the Britton wood institutes of the IMF and World Bank when it comes to loans, though the loans differ as the Britton wood institutes have conditional loans that meet certain criteria, the Chinese have ignored these rules of engagement though they have brought a new way where resources have been mortgaged for loans in some cases. The late Zambian President Edgar Lungu an authoritarian in his day was lavished in 2020 with a private jet by China a show that the Chinese are willing to spoil whoever is willing to give them mining rights in their country, in Lungu`s time they was an increase of Chinese mining investment in Zambia with reports of abuse of workers by the Chinese. Issues of democracy and accountability have been ignored by Chinese loans as seen in the relation between the Chinese and the fallen Rajapaksa dynasty which was blamed for mismanaging the Sri Lankan economy leading the country in to a crisis; Chinese loans were among the grievances of Sri Lankans. They have been reports in the past where money was said to have been channeled straight into the account of the then DRC`s president family accounts. Chinese borrowers have been accused for not following on how the loans were used and these have become haven for corrupt African politicians.

CHAPTER 2.
ZIMBABWE-CHINA RELATIONS

Zimbabwe-China Relations come a long way from the ideological relationships during the Cold War though China got read of the ideological relations in 1979 as it looked to solve its internal problems. Zimbabwe though adopting Communism upon gaining independence replaced it with Western ideologies of governance. The early 2000`s marked a different turn in the relations between Zimbabwe and China as Zimbabwe`s relationship with the West turned sower after the fall out between the Mugabe administration and the Blair administration in the UK. The Land Reform Program was the Trojan horse that was answered by sanctions on Zimbabwe the heaviest being ZIDERA by the United States of America. Mugabe then turned east launching a policy he termed the Look East policy, this policy, this policy was timely as the Hu Jintao administration(2003-2012) in China began to adopt an all-directional foreign policy that theoretically does not differ among geographical regions (Yun Sun 2014). The Chinese policy has not focused only on economical gained as the narrative is paddled among Western nations but it has roots in security, political and infrastructural developments with China having built most of the major soccer stadiums in Africa. The Look East policy yielded results fast as the Chinese investors began to come to Zimbabwe at a time the country had lost many Western companies due to sanctions. They was excitement among the locals who thought the Chinese were an angel of light, in 2007 I was a High School student when the mining company that had given the breath of life in Shurugwi for almost 50 years was acquired by the Chinese mining conglomerate SINO Steel. Indeed Zimbabwe had traded an old weak devil for a young hungry one as seen by the environmentally unfriendly mining that followed which left many scars to the once Scenic place Shurugwi was. The Chinese takeover was met with jubilation by the underground mine workers mainly the lowly paid as the new owners came criticizing the high salaries and car allocation scheme for management, six years down the line the company started to collapse and 2014 workers were given retirement packages and the rest is history. China Zimbabwe trade however has grown from lips and bounce as China is now one of Zimbabwe`s major trading partners and a source of investment according to a former President Mnangagwa advisor and political economist Eddie Cross over 80000 Chinese nationals now live in Zimbabwe a statement which the Spokesman of the Ministry of Information Nick Mangwana denounced as a lie (The Standard 2025). In 2023 it is projected two ways trade between the two countries reached a record high of $3.12 billion, with a 30% year on year increase (Herald online 2024). The discovery of Lithium in Zimbabwe strengthened the relationship between the two nations as Chinese companies are heavily involved in lithium production in Sandawana Mberengwa, Acturas near Harare and Bikita in Masvingo Province to name a few. In 2013 the Chinese government and Zimbabwe government managed to sign a deal that would see China build a parliament for Zimbabwe and the Chinese have not fallen sort of delivery as in 2023 the building was officially opened after completion. They have been complaints of China being involved in internal politics in Zimbabwe as seen with the military coup of November 2017 taking place after the then Commander of the Defense forces Constantine Chiwenga had come from China. Allegations of weapons being given for mineral concessions have also arisen as Zimbabwe has at many times received military hardware from China which includes guns, military jets and tankers.

Locals view of the Chinese

Shurugwi like most mining towns in Zimbabwe has been graced by mainly European mining companies which usually would run without the involvement of white Europeans in management level, but the Chinese have brought a new style where everyone in management is Chinese and the locals are the low income hard laborers. The Chinese model in the open cast mines in Wandara, Hilltop (Chidoor), Boterekwa, Showbread, Peak Mine, Camperdown and Bonza to name a few places have not been popular with locals as the workers work odd shifts with excavator operators working from 4 am to 10 pm and in some instance till 2 pm. The Chinese are famous for not paying locals good remuneration and in some instances have failed to pay and they have been allegations where they are said to tell workers that your government told us they is free labor in Zimbabwe. The Chinese have not bought or taken a mine which was not productive but mines where locals would have been mining high samples, locals seating in bars you will over hear saying Chinese are now making us their geo techs as we search for gold then chased in the event where a lot of it is found. Many black locals have a disdain for the Chinese investors as they lack respect for local traditions and view them as a threat to their livelihood which depends mostly on artisanal mining. The has been rumors where the Chinese have been accused of using force to buy mining claims from locals in the style that we see in their movies where the criminals gangs take territory by force it is said they have connections in the corridors of power and it is no rumor that Chengxi which owns most of the mines has one of President Emmerson Mnangagwa son as a director. In an incident where a local I interviewed called Clever was dismissed by the Chinese at Hilltop mine for wanting to attend his uncle`s funeral for several days, the employers so it as a wasting of days, from this I have drawn conclusion that the so called investors have no respect for our culture as long it comes in the way of their money. The use of heavy explosives has been a subject of contention among locals living near places the Chinese mine as the near sound and quaking during blasts worries locals that their houses will one day fall them, Shurugwi now differs not from Gaza and Ukraine when it comes to the sound of explosions something that was foreign in a peaceful Zimbabwe. Most of the grievances of the locals will be aired in the book mainly in the chapter showing the operations of the Chinese mining. Local business has become low as most places where artisanal miners used to mine now belong to the investor who uses machinery more than manual labor as means of production. However the Chinese presence have been beneficial to locals who have ball mills and hammer mills who are into the business of leaching gold through Cyanidation as the ore that artisanal miners pick from Chinese dumb has high quality of fine gold. Sex workers are another group of people that have benefitted as most of the Chinese are seen hanging around places where the oldest profession in the world is carried out like Melita and Vital Lounge. Local woman that have been married by the Chinese have been lavished by cars and other gifts, these ladies are now the new role models to young woman in a sea of poverty. The coming of Chinese has lowered the number murders among artisanal miners as they have security on the sites unlike in the past hooligans called Mabhuru used to control the trade by coercion. Chengxi also caught the eye of the ruling ZANU PF government as they have built offices for the part in Shurugwi. The Chinese have not bought or taken a mine which was not productive but mines where locals would have been mining high samples, locals seating in bars you will over hear saying Chinese are now making us their geo techs as we search for gold then chased in the event where a lot of it is found.

CHAPTER 3.
GOVERNMENT POLICIES

- **Indigenisation Policy:** The Zimbabwe government has been a victim of Western propaganda in some instance though it has also helped in creating this narrative, the Indigenization policy that was the brainchild of Robert Mugabe has been on paper one of the best policies in Africa that was meant to reverse the ills of colonialism. From Cape to Ouagadougou the cry has been the same whether it is Julius Malema or Ibrahim Traore all have borrowed from this masterpiece. The reincarnation of the Mines and Minerals Amendment Bill of 2007 as the Indigenization and Economic Empowerment Act of 2007 and the 2010 Regulations (Murombo Tumai 2010). The indigenization and Empowerment Act aimed to transfer 51% stake of all business with a net worth of $500000 to indigenous Africans, the policy aimed to create a business environment that ensured indigenous Zimbabweans benefit from natural resources. Large mining companies like UNKI mine that was owned by ANGLO America at that time were forced to build a processing plant in Shurugwi where they were mining rather than carrying the ore to South Africa thereby creating more job opportunities. In 2013 before the elections the Mugabe led ZANU PF came up with a program under the Ministry Youth Empowerment and Woman Development to give youths gold mining claims in Shurugwi. The policy has since lost steam as now most of the beneficiaries have sold the mining claims to the Chinese this can be attributed to lack of financing for locals to produce and personal greed of individuals. The indigenization policy also seemed as if it died with Mugabe as the gains are being reversed daily as locals lose the land to foreigners who have finances and are connected to the new dispensation of the 2nd Republic.
- **Environmental Management Act (Chapter 20:27):** This act is Zimbabwe`s primary legislation for environmental protection and sustainability. The agency has helped regulate mining activities in the country especially among artisanal miners that have no respect for laws.

  Below is a template from the Environment Management Agency that regulates mining activities:

ENVIRONMENTAL MANAGEMENT AGENCY

<u>ENVIRONMENTAL MANAGEMENT PLAN</u>

<u>FOR</u>

[*Provide Name(s) of project/District/Proponent details*]

....

....

1.0 INTRODUCTION

Zimbabwe is rich in mineral resources across the country particularly along the Great Dyke. As such a lot of mining activities are taking place by both large and small scale miners. The mining is also characterized by both legal and illegal miners with the highest number of illegal miners being constituted by small scale artisanal miners. However, the government has recognized that the artisanal and small scale mining sector is contributing more than half of the gold recorded so far and such the sector has the potential to stimulate economic growth and increase in the gross domestic product (GDP). Mining is an economic activity historically associated with many negative impacts such as environmental degradation, forced labor, child labor, and water pollution and over exploitation of natural resources. Despite these effects, small scale miners cannot be ignored due to their important contribution to the economy, employment, foreign currency generation.

Currently majority of the small scale miners are operating without Environmental Impacts Assessment (EIA) Certificates which is a violation of the Environmental Management Act Cap 20:27 and its ancillary legislation. One of the reasons cited by the small scale miners in terms of complying with the said legislation is lack of financial resources to undertake the EIA process. Some of the miners with EIA certificates are failing to comply with the submitted Environmental Management Plans (EMPs) mainly because of lack of understanding of the full contents of the so called "voluminous" EIA documents.

In order to improve compliance, it is proposed that small scale miners should be accommodated by way of assisting them to develop a generic and simplified Environmental Management Plan .The Agency should develop operational guidelines for small scale miners in line with the provisions of the Act. These guidelines will reduce the cost of engaging EIA consultancies for undertaking EIA reports. It is also expected that the guidelines should be simplified to enable easy understanding by the small scale miners.

2.0 REGISTRATION DOCUMENTATION

I. Registration certificate from Ministry of Mines and Mining Development
II. Approved Siting of Works Plan
III. Consultation with the farm owner/land owner
IV. Project details template completion(Appendix 1 Attached)
V. Payment of EIA review fees @ $210.00
VI. An inspection should be carried out by EMA and other stakeholders

VII. An Environmental Impact Assessment certificate initially valid for two years. To be issued. The certificate would then be subject for annual renewal during the operation period of the project

VIII. Quarterly reports should then be submitted.(EMA to develop a template)

After submission of the above requirements, the Agency is supposed to do a site visit and verification.

3.0 Operational Guidelines

ISSUE	MITIGATION MEASURE	WHEN	MONITORING AGENCIES
Vegetation destruction	Confine vegetation clearance to mining areas Reforestation programmes to be undertaken by the miner (to have a plantation onsite)	During mining operations	EMA, Forestry Commission, RDC
Rehabilitation of mined areas	Progressive rehabilitation of mined areas Protection of the pits by either fencing or complete closure Warning signs to be put in place Put in place danger warning signs at appropriate areas	During the project cycle	EMA/Min of Mines and Mining Development
Livestock and wildlife entrapment	Fencing and or protection of shafts Fencing of the operational area	When the project commences	EMA/Min of Mines
ISSUE	**MITIGATION MEASURE**	**WHEN**	**MONITORING AGENCIES**
Veld fires	Construction of standard fireguards around the claims Have adequate fire fighting equipment Create and provide a register for trained fire fighters	Before the fire season	EMA, Forestry Commission, RDC, ZRP

Sanitation issues	Construction of proper and adequate toilets	Before the project commences	EMA/Ministry of Health
Waste management	Provision of waste receptacles and disposal facility	Before the project commences	EMA
Decommissioning of the mined	Completely rehabilitate all mined areas Production of a decommissioning plan to relevant authorities	At decommissioning	EMA/Min of Mines, RDC
Exposure to chemicals	No chemical usage is allowed	During operations	EMA/Ministry of Mines
Safety of workers	Provision of adequate PPE Provision of adequate and visible danger warning signs Systematic and timely blasting and use of noise producing equipment Provide pre-blasting warnings to nearby residents/communities	During operations	EMA/NSSA/Ministry of Mines
Water pollution	All water from old shafts to be tested before disposal. All underground water to meet the disposal parameter	During operations During operations	EMA/ZINWA/Ministry of Mines
Land disputes	All disputes to be resolved amicably Consultations to be done at the preliminary stages Continuous engagement required	Before and during project implementation Before and during project implementation During operations	EMA/Ministry of Mines/RDC/ZRP

EMA is expected to inspect the mine at decommissioning

Appendix 1: Project Details

Name of Company……………………………………………………………………

Full Names of Developer…………………………………………………………

Identification/Passport Number……………………………………………….…..

Physical Address………………………………………………………………..

Telephone Numbers………………………………………………………………

Email Address………………………………………………………………………

Project Name/Mine Name…………………………………………………………

Type of Mineral…………………………………………………………………….

Number of Blocks…………………………………………………………………

Physical Address of Project……………………………………………………...

Province………………………District………………………………Ward……… ……..

Contact Person on Site………………………………………………………………

Telephone Number at Site…………………………………………………………

- **Government bans handheld GPS use:** The issue of mining boundaries disputes has been a question of interest mainly among miners in Zimbabwe. As of 1st July 2025 the Ministry of Mines and Mining Development issued a landmark directive requiring all mining title holders to submit survey-grade coordinates for their claims (Mapuranga R 2025). The issue of handheld GPS`s has been a center of disputes as some people lost their land especially in communal areas during the Lithium rush of 2022 whereby unsuspecting villagers were told to send whatsapp locations from their fields where they were lithium deposits this was done in the name of bringing buyers to where they were, only to their surprise the next thing someone claims your field to be his mine one such area I heard this was in Mberengwa Sandawana. They have been cases of individuals who would claim to possess Executive Prospectors Orders from the President who would claim land to be theirs in case they were a gold rush. The policy has come as a relief to communal area residences who were victims of flight by night mining activities in their areas which would leave pits and dangerous chemicals that endanger their livestock. In Dombojena and Gutsaruzhinji a man who locals known as Sibanda would appear with papers for a mine whenever they was a gold rush in a village, in Gutsaruzhinji a village Philemon Matemera took him to court as they disputed on the boundaries as he claims his mine crossed through Matemera`s field. The new law has brought hope to many Zimbabweans in Communal areas.

Literature Review

In the first 5 months of 2025 China Africa trade hit $134.16 billion up by 12,5% compared to same figures last year, the figures were announced by China`s ambassador to Ghana Tong Defa, on June 19 on a press briefing in Accra (Ecofin Agency 2025). The growth trajectory however remains a mystery to the poverty stricken majority of Africans as the continent remains among the poorest per GDP despite having many natural resources. It is estimated that trade between Zimbabwe and China surged to US$1.9 billion in the first five months of 2025, marking an impressive growth rate of more than 18% compared to the same period last year (Editor 2025). The relationship between Zimbabwe and China trade saw another development in 2025 as the two parties sealed a $55 million Cooperation deal alongside a separate commitment for food aid amounting to about $6.9 million for Zimbabwe (Ecofin Agency 2025). The government has since the inception of the 2nd republic announced signing of major deals without them materializing on the ground in form of changing the livelihood of the poor Zimbabweans. Zimbabwe has the fifth largest reserves of lithium in the world which is an essential component of the rechargeable batteries used in cellphones and electric cars, in places like Shamva 90 km northeast of Harare the discovery of lithium came as an opportunity to artisanal miners (Matiashe F 2024) but the dominance of the Chinese in the industry has affected locals as lithium extracting licenses are beyond the reach of many locals. "Chinese mining ventures have led to widespread environmental degradation n, disregard for the cultural rights of host communities, and, many cases the violation of the country`s labor laws, often with apparent impunity" and at least 95% of the of these workers at Chinese mines are working under short term, fixed contracts with no medical aid, pension, or any other benefits required when retiring (Maguwu 2024). President Mugabe, quoted in the Southern Times 21-28 April 2012 said "Our resources must be exploited to benefit our own people. Do you think God is a fool for placing all these natural resources in our land (Njini F 2012)? Mugabe if he is watching the plundering of the Chinese in Zimbabwe today turns in his grave as his words seem no longer relevant in the face of the 2nd Republic. The Zimbabwe Finance Minister Mthuli Ncube in September 2022 made a shocking revelation in parliament when he claimed Zimbabwe owed China almost $2.6 billion, the loans which were mainly for mining, manufacturing, infrastructure, agriculture and health sectors (Zvinoira T 2022). In Zimbabwe the level of political polarization and economic patronage bred by the turmoil of more than two decades has brought intricate questions to the forefront often with allegations proven or unproven of political partisanship in the distribution of resources (Murombo T 2010). The above literature can be supported by the 2013 distribution of mining claims that were given to ZANU PF youths in Shurugwi, they is even a place called Mayouth at Wandara mine in Shurugwi because the place was given to ZANU PF youths and any perceived opposition supporting youth is not allowed to operate there. ZIMASCO was Zimbabwe`s largest Ferro chrome producer prior to 2016 the company owned 80% of Ferro chrome deposits in Zimbabwe which has now been reduced to 40% after they were ceded by the government (Makichi 2016). The deposits which were given to other investors mainly the Chinese have suffered from land degradation like Lalapanzi and other areas along the Shurugwi Zvishavane road. The ceding of the mining deposits on paper is the best as it increases production of the commodity however corruption has tainted the idea. The droughts and industrial collapse of Zimbabwe has forced most of the young population which could not get jobs to pan for alluvial and reef along Zimbabwe`s rivers and mountain slopes where gold deposits were discovered along Zimbabwe`s Great Dyke (Milne and Marongwe 1995). The 21st century has however seen a new breed of gold miners now termed artisanal miners as the trade has been legalized, this group of small scale miners have become a little organized as they operate from mining claims that are documented. The artisanal miners face a threat of the Chinese and it seems there day is coming to an end. Chinese companies have been characterized by abuse of workers throughout the African continent, Nelson Holding a Chinese mining company brought before court by its 69 workers for failure to pay its workers from January to September 2014 (Khupe A 2014). However the issue of failure to pay salaries has been practiced even by local companies as some government parastatals like Forest Commission pay workers back pays of 4 months this can be attributed to the economic hardships in the country. In a decisive move to bring order to disputes in the mining sector in Zimbabwe the Ministry of Mines through the Provincial Mining Director`s office in Gweru gave a notice signed by K Mlangeni clearly stating that only registered mine surveyors using survey grade instruments are now authorized to provide coordinate data for the country`s mining cadaster (Mapuranga R 2025). The issue of boundaries will always remain contentious as long as Executive Prospectors Orders are in place as the holders abuse them if a claim belonging to a local starts producing kilograms of gold as seen in the case of Sibanda in Dombojena Shurugwi.

CHAPTER 3.
CHINESE MINING SITES IN SHURUGWI

Peak mine

Peak mine at the height of ZIMASCO operating days boasted the biggest mining shaft in Shurugwi and deepest as the shaft was said to be 1200 meters deep. The shaft was the company`s main producer of chrome and buses and trains would be seen so often carrying people to work. In February 2025 the shaft which had been contracted to Mutemera of Chrome West has been closed and sealed due to operational expenses being high. The location was home to a standard stadium that has since been abandoned and now in sorry state.

Above: Picture of number 5 Peak Mine

The previous Western owners of ZIMASCO can be credited for the development of Shurugwi in to a town as they built infrastructures ranging from schools like Railblock Primary, Peak Mine Primary, Ironsides Primary, Parkinson High School and Chrome High School. Even the owners of UNKI mine who are Western have also built schools in Chironde, Boterekwa School and Impali Primary School yet the all whether Chinese friends have done nothing in this department but blasting during school hours and this disrupts learning as they mine very close to schools and residential areas. Peak mine has the worst plundering as mining is done everywhere in an anarchical way.

Picture Own Source: Peak Mine Chinese Mining

The mining sites that the Chinese are mining in Peak Mine some have been said to have belonged to a local miner and businessman Mr Muchenje who was forced to sale to the Chinese in 2023 his mine was doing well as he had been able to acquire a dumb truck and excavators to use in production. Mr Muchenje due to the mining business had been able to build a luxurious home for himself and him and his family had luxurious vehicle a scene that is popular among artisanal miners. The Mudzengi family is also another group of miners in Peak Mine that lost some of their land to the Chinese at Number 4 Peak Mine, a small hectares of the mine was left for them, this is due to the fact they have a long history of being supporters of the ruling ZANU PF, this family had mined at the peak site since the early 2000's their eldest son Pride happened to be my former classmate. From a life of humble beginning their exploits and success in the artisanal mining circles is revered mainly in Shurugwi oldest location Makusha they also have roots in the chieftainship of Nhema making them a royal of Shurugwi but the axe of the Chinese takeover knows no chieftainship. The

Environmental Management has been raped by the Chinese while least "the government binds the land like a wife whose husbands binds her for another man to abuse her". Excavators and dump trucks move every minute as they plunder the scenery in the peak area the soil being dumped the gold containing belts going to the heap leach beds and the rest is but a tale. They is also another side of Peak Mine where mining claims have been rented to the Chinese by ZIMASCO and in that area you do not find a black soul being given that privilege. Attempts to apply for the land has been done by many locals I know but to no fruition the statement being Peak Mine is off limits to the locals but only available to the Chinese and this is from the office of the chairman who is Chinese.

Damage of the infrastructure since the Chinese takeover of ZIMASCO in 2007 cannot be ignored as seen with the stadium below which used to host the Chamber of Mines games and the last time premier league football was in Shurugwi Nichruit Football club used to play home matches there. Famous Zimbabwean Paralympic runner Elliot Mujaji once embraced the stadium at the peak of his career and Zimbabwean football players live Kingston Rinomhota who ended his career playing in Sweden played in the stadium but all the history has gone the drain as 10 meters from the stadium gold panning is taking place. Local artisans due to the closing of mining spaces due to the Chinese takeover are now mining wherever a gold signal is detected.

Picture Own Source: What left of Peak Mine Stadium

Road and railway Infrastructure affected by mining

Above Left: Road mined by artisanal miners *Above Right: Railway road to Peak*

The coming of the Chinese investors has put more pressure on local miners who survived mainly on artisanal mining since the Zimbabwean economy has suffered greatly from corruption and so called illegal Western sanctions. With ZIMASCO retrenching people in 2014 Shurugwi lost a major employer so artisanal mining is the largest employer. The Chinese mining uses machinery they by cutting on human labor which in turn is hard on locals, the mining that is occurring at the above road shows the desperation of miners who have families to feed and bills to pay but no way to work. The railway line used to transport chrome and workers from Peak Mine to Railblock but now they is no more train and the infrastructure has begun to perish. The former Rhodesian Prime Minister once said "if we give Africans the country they would not be railway stations to talk about" and it`s sad we are leaving in that reality today. The site on the above left is worrisome as artisanal miners now mine towards the road, when I asked a security officer of J and P who was on site about this his answer was people are hungry.

Ironkop Mine

The mine is a claim belonging to ZIMASCO gold mining started when the area was rented out to Mr Zingoma a local miner who was a former employee, in 2017 with the change of the helm of government the place was then given to the powerful Sibanda who as far as locals are concerned is the most powerful gold mafias operating in Midlands province. Sibanda did no spend a long time there as he did not meet too much success. In the process of time local successful miner Vitalis Hapazari known as vital reached an agreement with ZIMASCO that would see him produce 600 tons of ore every day. In the article that I wrote in 2023 titled Chinese Funding:

A Curse to Africa: A Case of Shurugwi Zimbabwe I cited that time would tell if Vital would be spared among locals that have lost mining claims to the Chinese and November 2024 became his dooms day as his contract was cut and offered to the new darlings of the Zimbabwe mining the Chinese. Ironkop Mine is unique as its near residential areas 20 meters from the nearest residential area Ironkop and Ironsides the mining activities has led to an increase in pollution both air pollution and noise pollution from explosives. The leaching beds that the Chinese use are a threat even to the animals that used to habitat in the area like baboons that are now a site in Makusha and Ironsides as they look for food and sanctuary. They is a plot nearby owned by a Doctor Shoko who has goats and cattle and these may become victims of cyanide and other chemicals used in the Chinese heap leaching. The site of a dumb that is just across the road to Peak Mine from Shurugwi CBD, is an accident ready to happen if heavy rains are to fall, mountains have been destroyed and been replaced by artificial heaps of soil and the Environmental management Agency has been relegated to arresting firewood tree cutters as they cannot raise their voices to the mighty Chinese plunderers that are destroying forest as they will. Getting to the mining site you would imagine that mining has been taking place for a very long time yet it has only been seven months as shown in the pictures below you would wonder what will be the case if the mining company continues for another 5 years. They would not be a mountain to talk about, the Chinese mine as if they have a vendetta with mountains the land degradation is of the highest level, and surely human activities will end this planet.

Zimbabweans work Minimal Jobs only

The Chinese owners have Zimbabwean locals working as dumb truck operators and excavator drivers, the rest are security guides and dumb truck guides while the Chinese are management. A walk near the mine you will see sites of Chinese on motorbikes monitoring the locals as hawks monitoring chicken. If Tongogara would rise from his grave he would moan seeing how low black Zimbabweans have been reduced to. The late President Robert Mugabe once gave a speech where he cited that they invited the Chinese to partner with but they now bring even workers for minimal jobs. Our universities that teach management will not have students if the Chinese investors continue coming as they don’t believe in black managers as seen where they mine, the highest ranking local you find is an interpreter.

Ironkop Mine Pictures: Own Source

The dumb is in an area that is at the side of Tebekwe and in April they was a dispute with owner of Tebekwe mine Smelly Dube who thought the Chinese were encroaching in to her mine though the issue was later resolved. The mining dumbs are on an increase and are affecting the biodiversity of the forests where mining is taking place. Trees are covered with soil and these artificial mountains are springing everywhere in Shurugwi.

Hilltop Mine (Chidoor)

The Hilltop mine famously known as Chidoor was owned by Adonis Chipwanyira a local miner before its acquisition by Chinese investors who rumors said paid him $150000 to get the mine. The mine had saved as a haven for residents of Ironsides especially in 2008 when Zimbabwe underwent an economic crisis many people including civil servants survived by artisanal mining at the mine. The Hilltop mine since its takeover by the Chinese has been at the center of allegations as at one time they were forced to close for some days as they had blocked water that moves to the Dan Raven falls. The mine however has been of help to women artisanal miners who would not traditionally go underground to dig for gold as they were now going to mine dumps to look for debris of gold containing rocks which they would put in empty cement sacks and go with them to the ball mills to mill for gold. The artisanal who have suffered due to the hooligan groups like Baca who are famous for robbing people of rich ores of gold in the Great Dyke as the Chinese operations have brought heavy security presence to mining. The Chinese under Chengxi that mine at the

Hilltop like at every site in Shurugwi have had the privilege of having state security like the support unity famously known as the Black boots and neighborhood watch operating at this sites as security a development that has supported the allegation that the highest office in the land has shares in the mining activities. The support unity is Zimbabwe`s most elite polite force known for its no nonsense stance so they is order in the Chinese mines. Like at any other Chinese owned mine the issue of noise pollution through explosives is common at Hilltop mine, they has been a behavior last year and early this year where artisanal miners would run in to the area where a blast would have been carried out in order to pick gold bearing stones before the smoke settles, this poses a danger of people contacting silicosis tuberculosis from the gas emissions, but to tell this fact to hungry people your answer will be "what does not kill". Incidents of mistreatment of workers by the Chinese have been talked about by workers that I interviewed one of them called Clever was dismissed after asking for permission to attend a funeral of his uncle in Gokwe, he was offered a single day when the journey takes almost a day and when he tried to explain was told he can excuse himself from the job. An excavator driver called Vin was involved in an accident while driving a dump truck he blamed the incident on tiredness from working long working hours, the workers of the Chinese are sometimes forced to work overtime till 10 pm yet they are wanted the next day at work at 5 pm. The remuneration has been known not to meet the long hours of work with some Chinese being accused of telling locals you are lucky we pay you your government says they is free labor in Zimbabwe. Like other Chinese miners the Hilltop miners also practice heap leaching and it is a threat to cattle from farming arrears near the mining site like Jackfort farm and Gutsaruzhinji area. Before the open cast mining the place was known as njinji (a place where African plums grow) now the place has no site of a single tree this has created a new ecosystem of soil mountains. Baboons, monkeys and warthogs used to live in the area but have since migrated because of the noise pollution of blasts and human activities. The bio diversity has been affected and a problem of humans and monkeys scrapping for crops in Ironsides location which is near Hilltop mine is now a common occurrence. The roads to the mine are only dust unlike the British which build tarred roads the Chinese would rather buy cars fit for the terrain than build road infrastructure.

July 2025 Miracle

In the month of July 2025 it seemed as if the artisanal miners` gods had smiled on them as the Chinese suddenly moved their machinery from the Hilltop mine rumors suggesting they had moved to Shamva where they was a gold rush. They only left a single excavator and a single dumb truck mainly for their leaching pads. The problems that ensured now were the violence of the Mabhuru who were taking ores from the artisanal miners with the help of state security stationed at the place.

Above Picture: An open Cast left by Chinese where locals were now working in July-August 2025: Own Source

Artisanal Miners Working at Hilltop Mine in 2025

Artisanal miners working at an open cast left by the Chinese using minimal tools like hammers and chisels. The miners only mine mostly ore that can fit in an empty cement bag and it is rare for them to have ore exceeding 5 bags. These are mainly locals from surrounding areas; this picture was taken in August 2025. They mine as individuals or in syndicates which have no formal organization, they are prone bullying and robberies from the police and Mabhuru gangs operating in Shurugwi like the Mashabani, Baca and other groups. These miners mill their ore at ball mills near Hilltop or if they are sponsored by other individuals with ball mills away from the area transport are provided to carry the ore. The miners how ever have a challenge in mining when the Chinese are operating as they do not allow them access to working sites they are therefore left with the option of scavenging

Wonderful Group of Mines

The mine is known among many locals as Wandara and this is by size the biggest gold mining deposit in Shurugwi. The Germans are rumored to have mined in this place for a period and they are said to have left in the period from 1950 to 1958 this is evidenced by the presence of many tunnels that they are found in places where the Germans mined. The German shafts as they are known have been as source of living for most people in Shurugwi as the miners mine pillars that were left behind and low sample gold riff belts that were left. Mining at Wandara has its dangers as the mining of pillars have meant the weakening of the shafts as some have collapsed and killed people in the past. Besides the miners the most successful gold dealers and miners in Shurugwi have built there fortune from Wandara these includes Nicholas Gara a renowned businessman who own a lodge called Nichruit, Chimona who is a ZANU PF central committee member, Vital who owns most business in Shurugwi town among many. The source of wealth at Wandara for locals has been ball mills as the ore is said to be rich with gold for leaching using Cyanidation. A visit to Wandara in the past would be met with the sound of ball mills as this is Shurugwi ball mill center is they was such, the gold has a high percentage ranging from 93% and above. The coming of the Chinese to the place means more than a thousand people that have their livelihood there, are under threat. The Chinese take over started with acquisition of a place called Mupenzeni and other areas followed, they have been rumors that as of September 2025 the locals have been told to vacate the whole area. Areas like Mayouth where most people had ball mills and where many used to mine if people are to move would shake businesses in Shurugwi and may result in increase in crime rate. However the Chinese have been able to level certain places that were dangerous to mine through their use of excavators. The road to Wandara is dust road a character of the Chinese lack of commitment to road infrastructural development in places where they invest, the local workers stay in small wooden cabins and is not allowed to bring spouses, a concept that has taken our locals to the days of colonialism where man lived away from their families. Gender in the work place has been another problem with Chinese mining as women are not incorporated even for jobs that are traditionally for women like cooking and cleaning showing they no regards for gender laws of the land where woman participation is encouraged in all sectors of the economy. Wandara has been a haven for Mabhuru and its Chinese total take over signals disaster in the remaining black owned mines. Wandara has also provided a livelihood for people who operate small tuck shops (Chibhongashuro) that sell food items to the miners, another business that has benefitted from the area was the transport business from providing transport from Shurugwi town to the area and dumb trucks carrying ore from the mining areas to mills, boiler a tanks among others. Wandara since the closure of operations at ZIMASCO Shurugwi has been the single largest employer of people in Shurugwi and its Chinese takeover warranties the town to be a ghost town.

Ball mills at Wandara Mayouth area

The ball mill as its name suggest is a machine that uses big round iron balls that are put in the basin area shown on the above picture, milling takes about 90 minutes for the stones to be completely crushed. One compartment of the ball mill can take 1 bag of empty cement with ore so the one above can take ore from two bags at the same time. The ball mills are a common machine where artisanal miners operate as they are cheap and easy to operate.

Boterekwa

Land degradation

Boterekwa pass is a stretch of road in Shurugwi stretching 6 km of terrain that is hard to navigate for drivers. The pass earned Shurugwi its nickname the Scenic Shurugwi because of the beauty of the mountains. Local miners since years preceding 2010 and beyond have enjoyed success in the gold mining trade with people like Chris Mahara, Harold, Ticha Darangwa, Chamu Mahwanda, Stoddard and R. G Godard to name a few having acquired a fortune from there. The mining claims in the area had always been government reserves until the day of the 2nd Republic of President Emmerson Mnangagwa which has seen the majority of the local miners being bought out of the area in a mafia style by a Chinese company Chengxi. "The mining company has not been merciful to the environment in Boterekwa as land degradation at a level we have not experienced as a nation since the day Cecil John Rhodes defeated the Ndebele amabutho in 1896", these were the words of former ZANU PF central committee member for Mashonaland West Bombshell Geza on an YouTube live video. As I have indicated before it seems the Chinese dislike Mountains. The Environmental Management Agency (EMA) have become a toothless bulldog in the face of the Chinese being relegated to an organization which only has power when it comes to locals that cut firewood. An EMA manager who was stationed at the Shurugwi District office was rumored to have written a memo on the activities of the Chinese destruction of the environment to his superiors in the Capital Harare, the next thing he was promoted to Gokwe where they is no gold showing that the organization`s capacity to implement its powers as enshrined in the constitution were limited. Excavators at Boterekwa have brought destruction at a rate never seen in the town the site seem as if it has been mined for decades. The former Scenic place has become scarred and surrounded by artificial mountains of soil. The British use to mine inclined shafts where you would not see the damage of the environment but Zimbabwe`s all weather friends have no respect for the environment. In the picture on the next page you will see a couple of trees that are not indigenous these were planted by the Chinese during their first days of operation but now they do as they please as they are now the law.

Below Boterekwa land degradation: Picture Own Source

The heaps seen in the picture of loose soil are left without vegetation rehabilitation changing the outlook of the forest and the whole place. Years after the mining if action is not taken this will become the natural habitat of the place.

Above Mining Done Directly on top of Main road: Picture Own Source

Huge blasts carried out at the site sometimes cover the road with a cloud of dust that can disrupt vehicles till the cloud clears. In case a loose rock is blasted in the air it can prove disastrous if it moves to the direction of the road a fact the plunderers don't seem to care about. They is not even a warning siren before blasting it is done as the mining company schedules without alerting the public.

Heap leach Cyanidation plant in Boterekwa

The Cyanidation plant is the most important place in the operation at Boterekwa and the plant is heavily guarded with gun yielding police and security along with the Chinese. The plant is a no go area for many people as it is where the final product is produced unlike other gold mines where fidelity come to take gold here gold is collected by cars from a small motorcade. The plant is however a threat to the residents of Msasa and their cattle as water from the pads spill during rainy season. A video was once leaked on social media where a lot of gold was been shown and the person recorded on video was saying the gold was from Boterekwa. Despite all these exploits of gold Shurugwi remains a small town with little development whilst gold is being milked from it to China. The operation in Boterekwa has been alleged like all other operations to have the first family`s hand.

Local Artisanal Miners livelihood

The black locals and the animals whose livelihood survived on Boterekwa are victims of Chinese investment in the form of never been involved in the process of the mining developments. Before the Chinese when they were multiple owners of claims in Boterekwa pass many black locals mined there but since the Chinese took over only the skilled dumb truck and excavator operators have benefitted living the rest of the people as scavengers. Artisanal miners would come from Nhema which is the rural district of Shurugwi and the urban area to mine belts but the new owners have come up with a barbaric proposal where locals are allowed to word at night from 2 am to 5 am and this type of arrangement has come with dangers in form of Mabhuru where the miners are mainly robbed of ore at the nearby road since it will be dark when they knock off. People like Clair and the Majengwa boys of Ironsides Shurugwi have made names for themselves in this arrangement as they have asserted themselves as authorizes as they are known for bullying other miners and for taking their ore. Security has not been provided for the locals and they have been incidents where rocks have almost fallen on people as they work a man from Gutu named Nigel Yourgen once narrated to me how he almost got squashed by a boulder of rock only to be drawn out of the way by a friend. The local artisanal miners claim that the Chinese work from 12 am to 2 am to close the belts with boulders so that when the locals come at 2 am they don't have access to ore as they spend time trying to remove the rocks. Some locals with connections have had access to the mining site by paying the security so that they can mine and when the Chinese are on their way they may alert them so they can escape. The locals both the security and the artisanal miners have blended in order to survive in an anarchical situation where the color of skin and the political position guaranties you food on the table. Being injured in these types of mining can be dangerous as no one compensate you. Kudakwashe Mberengwa whom I once interviewed was beaten by security in Boterekwa when he was caught at the mining site though he was not mining; he sustained injuries that made him not to walk for 3 weeks in 2023.

Type of ore at Boterekwa

Above Picture of gold bearing ore: Own Source

Like every other place where artisanal mining is carried out the miners are seen with small empty cement bags for ores. The ore mined in Boterekwa is famously known as the red oaks belt which derives its name from the color of the soil found near the belt. The miners claim that the ore is good for Cyanidation hence the lines of cars to transport the miners in the morning to the milling bases, as the owners of the cars require the sands left after free gold has been extracted from the rock. The above ore stone in very hard to crash so a ball mill is very ideal to use. The ore in Boterekwa like at Wandara has a high percentage of gold also hence the higher the number of artisanal miners you find at the awkward 2 am shift an estimated number of 500 people work at the place at night.

CHAPTER 4.
INFRASTRUCTURAL DEVELOPMENT IN SHURUGWI.
FACILITIES BUILT BY MINING COMPANIES IN SHURUGWI

ZIMASCO has been part of the Shurugwi story for more than 50 years since its formation and the mining company has been able to develop the town in to what it is today with 6 locations including Ironsides, Peak mine, Railblock, Ironkop, Mambowa and Musgrave in Shurugwi town the company literary built the town. Schools have been constructed in those years which include Peak Mine Primary School, Rail Block Primary School, Ironsides Primary School and Parkinson High School showing a commitment from the company to change the lives of children in the town. With the Railblock hospital and several clinics the company did more for the community than even the government of the days it has operated. But ZIMASCO damage to the environment has been lesser than the development it has brought with 3 mining portals in Shurugwi including Peak Mine, Rail Block and Ironton. In the 4 years that the Chinese presence in Shurugwi they has not been any development on infrastructure not even pills in hospitals except a ZANU PF office building. The Chinese even go to the extent of having their workers living in small one room wooden cabins that are temporary structures they can remove when they decide to live. Another Western company that has done wonders is UNKI mine who has been able to develop a location of their own called Impali; the company has invested in high rising apartments that have made the location attractive to independence land developers and new independent home owners. UNKI has also like ZIMASCO invested in schools having built Impali Primary School, Chironde High School and Boterekwa School these social cooperate responsibilities from the mine has come in hand to the Shurugwi community. The Chinese investors have shown little or no interest in cooperate social responsibilities but are mainly focused on mining without giving back.

Pictures of Schools built by Mining Companies in Shurugwi

Parkinson High School: Picture Own Source

Ironsides Primary School: Picture Own Source

Road Infrastructure

The Germans, British and locals are credited for building most of the roads in Shurugwi. The Boterekwa pass is one masterpiece that leaves every one that passes through it in marvel of how the Germans built the road. The town unlike other small mining towns in Shurugwi has the best roads and they have been maintained by the big mining companies operating in the area. In 2024 the ANGLO America run UNKI mine at the time helped revamp the road form the Government Complex to Parkinson High School which was in bad shape, the Chinese at the other hand prefer buying new cars that navigate hard terrains like the Toyota Hilux GD6 than fixing roads. UNKI mine built also a 15 km road to Chironde where the mine operates from and also another road to Impali whilst the Chinese operate from areas with dust roads.

Boterekwa road built by the Germans

CHAPTER 5.
CONCLUSION

The relationship between China and Zimbabwe which has a deep root in the political arena and strong history between the two nations is a bond that is to be revised especially in light with the damage shown by this book. Foreign investment in the mining sector though historically in Shurugwi, Zimbabwe has brought about development and opportunities in the case of the Chinese it has brought damage to the environment at a cost that locals and environmentalists see as having a negative impact as shown in the book. With government policies only being good on paper without a proper follow up due to corrupt government officials and greediness it will be hard to save the environment from the Chinese onslaught. The leaving out of communities in making major developments in their areas due to the centralization of decisions in Zimbabwe mean the locals can be abused by foreign investors without them having a chance to fight against such. The deposition of loose soil on dumbs that are close to roads like in Boterekwa and Ironkop are hazards that need attention if disaster is to be avoided in case if heavy rains and cyclones are to be experienced within the region. Protection of local claim holders is something that ought to be looked on in order to save them from greed political elites. This work is a voice of communities that cannot stand against rogue elements of investment as it brings in focus the reality hidden from most Zimbabweans who do not live in mining towns. Infrastructural development should be the centre of every foreign investment that is to be carried in Zimbabwe so as the locals can remain with gains if the mining companies decide to leave as shown with the development brought to Shurugwi by ZIMASCO. Every mining company operating in Zimbabwe should work to preserve the bio diversity rather than plunder. Competition from both the East and West should not bully the local mining companies in to submission as they are the first line of investment and custodians of the land. Botswana has followed investment policies that has the Batswana benefiting directly from the mining and are protected from abuse Zimbabwe ought to follow such a path if meaningful economic development is to take place. Places like Wandara mine that service many people in a country where the industry has collapsed must not be totally given to foreign investors who do not create jobs for the locals as their livelihood should be prioritized above an investment for a nation which does not invest in its people is an enemy of its people in the long run. The Environmental Management Agency (EMA) must be allowed to do its job without political influence and selective use of the law for no one is above the constitution. The mining method that has been practiced for a long time in Shurugwi has been the inclined shaft mining; the mining method has helped create jobs an example being ZIMASCO and UNKI mine who have a lot of workers however the

Chinese prefer open cast mining where the only workers are excavator and dumb truck operators, job creation has not been an integral part of China`s mining investment in Shurugwi hence the disdain of the Chinese in Shurugwi. Job creation was one of the campaign promises of President Mnangagwa`s campaign in the 2023 presidential election so Chinese mining has gone against the promise as they bring even low labor workforce from China who monitor the excavators and dumb trucks something a local can do. There is need for strengthening regulations and ensuring accountability among investors are crucial for balancing economic benefits with environment and social protection. Transparency, community engagement and environmental safeguards are essential for sustainable mining practices. The issue of platinum and lithium being forced to be processed in Zimbabwe shows how African governance are now seeking to maximize benefits from foreign investments. There should be a balance between profiteering and socio-economic developments by foreign investors. The use of machinery that replaces human labor without safeguarding jobs for locals should be regulated so that locals are not affected. African governments should put in place laws that allow for locals to occupy positions of influence in foreign companies operating in their countries.

REFERENCES

Bloomberg. ZIMASCO. Global Infrastructure Magazine. www.zimasco.co.zw .2010

Ecofin Agency. Zimbabwe and China Seal $55 million Cooperation Deal, Strengthening Ties in Development and Trade. The Zimbabwean. August 2025.

Ecofin Agency. China-Africa Trade Hits $134.16 billion, Up 12.4% in First Five Months. www.ecofinagency.com. June 2025.

Editor. Zimbabwe-China Trade Hits US$1.9 billion in Five Months. hurumende.com . July 2025

Maguwu F. Troubles Mount with Chinese Mining In Zimbabwe. DAILY NEWS. April 2025

Makichi T. ZIMASCO cedes chrome claims to government. The Herald. April 16

Mapuranga R. Zimbabwe Moves to End Mining Boundary Disputes with Mandatory Survey-Grade Coordinates: Government Bans Handheld GPS Use. July 2025.

Matiashe F. As China Scrambles for Zimbabwe`s lithium, small miners are left behind. Aljazeera. June 2024.

Milne G R and Marongwe D A. Small Scale Gold Panning in Zimbabwe, Economic Costs, Benefits and Poling Recommendations: Results of a pilot study in Mashonaland Central for 1993. 1995.

Moyo P, Chivivi O, Mapuwei N, Masuku C. Press and Environmental Management Agency (EMA`s) Active role in Reporting and Monitoring Environmental Degradation Caused by Small Scale Artisanal Gold Panning in Zimbabwe A Case of Shurugwi Peri Urban. Journal of Environmental and Earth Science. 2015

Murombo T. Law and the Indigenisation of mineral resources in Zimbabwe: Any equity for local communities? 25 SAPL. 2010

.Zvinoira T. The Strange ale of China` loans to Zimbabwe. Newsday. September 2022.

www.ingramcontent.com/pod-product-compliance
Lightning Source LLC
LaVergne TN
LVHW051131210926
848482LV00001B/55
9798899664656